This new edition of the N............................
to-date information abo...........................
public transport and othe................ ... ..miles of the
North Downs Way Nation.. .... .. Surrey and Kent. It should help
in planning anything from a long distance walking holiday requiring
overnight accommodation to an afternoon out with a call at the local
pub.

Like the earlier edition, this guide does not aim to be a directional
guidebook to the route itself: for this information reference should
be made to the North Downs Way National Trail Guide by Neil Curtis
(Aurum Press, £8.99). There are a number of information leaflets
about aspects of the North Downs Way, including circular walks
leading from it into the surrounding countryside; these are listed on
page 5.

CONTENTS

Introduction	3
Who can use the North Downs Way?	4
Finding the Way	4
Ordnance Survey Maps	4
Guides	5
Other Long Distance Routes	6
Tourist Information	8
Police and Ambulance	8
Useful Addresses	9
Bus Services	12
Rail Services	12
Facilities and Accommodation	13
Key to Maps	13
Maps	14
Youth Hostel Association - The place to stay	40
Index of Places	42
The Country Code	44

INTRODUCTION

Opened officially in 1978 and running for 153 miles/245km across Surrey and Kent, the North Downs Way is one of ten or so National Trails in England and Wales and as such is among the most important routes in Britain for informal countryside recreation.

Although some other National Trails may offer more rugged and isolated surroundings, the North Downs Way makes up for this in the sheer variety of settings through which it passes. From open grassland to shady woods, hilltop churches to historic towns, orchards to the Channel clifftops, the range is enormous. A journey on the North Downs Way provides plenty of opportunities to understand and enjoy the landscape, agriculture, wildlife and history of the area.

Recently plans have been developed to link the North Downs Way at Otford with the eastern end of the new Thames Path National Trail at Greenwich. The North Downs Way is also being twinned with part of the Grande Randonnée system in France, providing many exciting opportunities for long distance walking. More details can be found on page 7.

Inevitably the modern world has an impact upon the National Trail in various ways, such as motorways and Channel Tunnel facilities. However, if your need to cross the region requires less speed and more quiet enjoyment then the North Downs Way provides a means of doing so. It is hoped that this guide will help those using it to get the most out of this attractive and historic route.

WHO CAN USE THE NORTH DOWNS WAY?

The North Downs Way is mainly intended to be a route for use by walkers. It may be walked from end to end or in sections, either as part of a circular walk or, in many areas, by the planned use of public transport.

It is wise to be prepared for the elements: even in the summer wind and rain can make a walk cold and uncomfortable, so suitable warm and waterproof clothing should be worn or carried in a small rucksack. Some sections of the route may be muddy, especially in the winter, so stout footwear is advisable.

In some locations the North Downs Way runs along rights of way which are bridleways (which may be used by horseriders and pedal cycles) or byways (which are open to all traffic). Generally the waymarking will indicate the precise status of any particular section of the route.

FINDING THE WAY

The National Trail symbol is an acorn, and it is to be found on a variety of waymarks along the North Downs Way, including wooden pointers, metal finger posts and small circular emblems attached to stiles, fences or free-standing posts. In Kent there are also a number of older stone plinths.

It should be possible to follow the route in either direction entirely by reference to the waymarking, but enjoyment will be increased if appropriate maps and one of the North Downs Way guides are used - see page 5.

ORDNANCE SURVEY MAPS

1:50,000 (Landranger Series)

Sheets 186 (Aldershot, Guildford & area), 187 (Dorking, Reigate & Crawley), 188 (Maidstone & The Weald of Kent), 178 (The Thames Estuary), 189 (Ashford & Romney Marsh), 179 (Canterbury & East Kent).

1:25,000 (Pathfinder Series)

Sheets 1225 (SU84/94), 1226 (TQ04/14), 1206 (TQ05/15), 1207 (TQ23/32), 1208 (TQ45/55), 1193 (TQ66/76), 1209 (TQ65/75), 1230 (TQ84/94), 1210 (TQ85/95), 1226 (TR04/14), 1211 (TR05/15), 1212 (TR25/35), 1252 (TR3/23), 1232 (TR24/34).

These maps show rights of way, although there may be errors or omissions in some instances. Ordnance Survey maps are obtainable from good bookshops or Ordnance Survey Agents.

GUIDES

North Downs Way National Trail Guide by Neil Curtis. Aurum Press

Walk the North Downs by John Hawell. John Bartholomew & Sons.

Discovering the North Downs Way by David J Allen & Patrick R Imrie Shire Publications

Walking the North and South Downs by Mark Chapman. Hale

Long Distance Paths - South East England by Alan Castle. Black

A Guide to the Pilgrim's Way and North Downs Way by Christopher John Wright. Constable.

Explore the Pilgrim's Way by Alan Charles. Countryside Books

The Pilgrim's Way in Kent by Donald Maxwell. Kent Messenger (reprint of 1932 booklet).

All of the above books were in print at the time of going to press. In addition, the 1982 guide The North Downs Way by Denis Herbstein (H.M.S.O.) may still be available, but contains some outdated information.

The following leaflets and information packs are published by the North Downs Way Project at Kent County Council. They are available in some bookshops and tourist information centres, or from the Countryside Group, Planning Department, Kent County Council, Springfield, Maidstone, Kent ME14 2LX, Tel Maidstone (0622) 696168.

North Downs Way Circular Walks -

Maidstone area (pack of 4 leaflets)	£1.20
Canterbury area (pack of 4 leaflets)	£1.20
Between Harrietsham and Wye	
(single leaflets being published during 1994)	30p each

North Downs Way - Historic Churches   Free

North Downs Way - Wildlife   Free

On Foot from the Thames to the North Downs   Free

Walks from London to Paris   Free
  (pack of leaflets including On Foot
  from the Thames to the North Downs)

OTHER LONG DISTANCE ROUTES

THE GREENSAND WAY
The Greensand Way runs for 168km (105 miles) from Haslemere in Surrey to Hamstreet in Kent, where it joins the Saxon Shore Way. There are links between the North Downs Way and the Greensand Way in several places: **1.** Moor Park (east of Farnham) to Thursley; **2.** Guildford to Shamley Green (following the Downs link); **3.** Ranmore Common (west of Dorking) to Westcott; **4.** Colley Hill (near Reigate) to Skimmington; **5.** South Hawke (near Oxted) to Oxted Mill; **6.** North of Westerham to Westerham village; **7.** North of Charing to Charing village.

The Greensand Way in Surrey - A Walker's Guide. Surrey County Council (available from Public Relations Unit, County Hall, Kingston upon Thames, Surrey KT1 2DN).

The Greensand Way in Kent. Kent County Council (available from Access and Recreation Officer, Planning Department, KCC, Springfield, Maidstone, Kent ME14 2LX).

THE DOWNS LINK
This is a 48km (30 miles) route linking the North Downs Way at St Martha's Hill, near Guildford, Surrey with the South Downs Way at Steyning, West Sussex. A leaflet is available from Public Relations Unit, Surrey County Council, County Hall, Kingston upon Thames, Surrey KT1 2DN.

THE WEALDWAY
The Wealdway runs for 129km (80 miles) from Gravesend in Kent to Eastbourne in East Sussex, crossing the North Downs Way near Trottiscliffe. It also links with the South Downs Way.

The Wealdway Guide by Geoffrey King. Wealdway Steering Group (c/o 11 Old London Road, Brighton, East Sussex BN1 8XR).

A Guide to the Wealdway by John H Mason. Constable.

There are a number of other regional routes which cross or link with the North Downs Way. The Saxon Shore Way, from Gravesend in Kent to Rye in East Sussex, is currently undergoing a programme of refurbishment. The Darent Valley Path runs from Dartford to Sevenoaks, crossing the North Downs Way at Otford. The Stour Valley Walk crosses the National Trail at Wye and Canterbury. A newly-opened extension to the Elham Valley Path links with the North Downs Way near Barham and Canterbury. For details of these routes and publications, contact the Access and Recreation Officer, Planning Department, Kent County Council, Springfield, Maidstone, Kent ME14 2LX.

WALKS FROM LONDON TO PARIS
Two projects linking the North Downs Way with other long distance routes have created a means of walking between the capital cities of the UK and France, a total distance of 710km (445 miles).

During 1994 the North Downs Way is being twinned with parts of the Grande Randonnée system of long distance paths in France. The route in question follows the coast path from Calais to Etaple, then strikes inland and southwards through a variety of scenery, passing historic sites such as the battlefield at Crécy. It enters Paris from the west by way of the Bois-de-Boulogne.

At the same time a link has been devised between the North Downs Way at Otford and the eastern end of the new Thames Path National Trail at the Thames Barrier, by way of the Darent Valley Path and a number of waymarked recreational routes in the Boroughs of Bexley, Bromley and Greenwich. When the Thames Path is fully open in 1996, it will be possible to walk from the source of the river in Gloucestershire to the Thames Barrier, a distance of 288km (180 miles).

A number of publications have been produced to promote these links: see Guides (page 6).

For further details contact the Countryside Group, Planning Department, Kent County Council, Springfield, Maidstone, Kent ME14 2LX.

TOURIST INFORMATION

There are Tourist Information Centres at the following places close to the North Downs Way:

Farnham Vernon House, 28 West Street, Farnham, Surrey GU9 7BR
Tel: (0252) 715109

Guildford The Undercroft, 72 High Street, Guildford, Surrey GU1 3HE
Tel: (0483) 444007

Sevenoaks Buckhurst Lane, Sevenoaks, Kent TN13 1LQ
Tel: (0732) 450305

Rochester Eastgate Cottage, High Street, Rochester, Kent ME1 1EW
Tel: (0634) 843666

Maidstone The Gatehouse, Old Palace Gardens, Mill Street, Maidstone, Kent ME15 6YE
Tel: (0622) 673581/602169

Canterbury 34 St Margaret's Street, Canterbury, Kent CT1 2TG
Tel: (0227) 766567

Folkestone Harbour Street, Folkestone, Kent CT20 1QN
Tel: (0303) 58594

Dover Burlington House, Townwall Street, Dover, Kent CT16 1JR
Tel: (0304) 205108

POLICE AND AMBULANCE

In emergency dial 999 and ask for the service required. To contact local police stations, telephone the number relevant to the County you are in and you will be put through.

Surrey (0483) 571212
Kent (0622) 690690

USEFUL ADDRESSES

All Wheel Drive Club   30 Tilbury Road, Rainham, Kent ME8 7QA
                              Tel: (0634) 375037

British Horse Society   Primrose Lodge, Duddleswell, Uckfield,
                              East Sussex TN22 3JN
                              Tel: (082 571) 2689

**British Trust for   36 St Mary's Street, Wallingford, Oxon
Conservation Volunteers**   OX10 0EU Tel: (0491) 39766
                              Kent Office, c/o Planning Department, Kent
                              County Council, Springfield, Maidstone, Kent
                              Tel: (0622) 696413
                              Surrey Office, Highway House,
                              21 Chessington Road, West Ewell,
                              Surrey KT17 1TF
                              Tel: 081 541 7157

**Byways & Bridleways   The Granary, Charlcutt, Calne,
Trust**   Wilts SN11 9HL
                              Tel: (024 974) 273

**Council for the Protection Warwick House, 25 Buckingham Palace Rd,
of Rural England**   London SW1W 0PP
                              Tel: (071) 976 6433
                              The Oast, Coldharbour Farm, Wye,
                              Ashford, Kent TN25 5DB

Countryside Commission   HQ, John Dower House, Crescent Place,
                              Cheltenham, Glos GL50 3RA
                              Tel: (0242) 521381
                              S.E. Regional Office, 71 Kingsway,
                              London WC2B 6ST
                              Tel: 071 831 3510

Cyclists Touring Club   69 Meadow, Godalming, Surrey GU7 3HS
                              Tel: (0483) 417217

English Heritage   Fortress House, 23 Savile Row,
                              London W1X 1AB
                              Tel: (071) 973 3000

English Nature	Kent: Coldharbour Farm, Wye, Ashford, Kent TN25 5DB Tel: (0233) 812525
	Surrey: Old Candlemakers, West Street, Lewes, East Sussex BN7 2NZ Tel: (0273) 474595
Forest Enterprise	Weald Forest District Office, Goudhurst, Cranbrook, Kent TN17 2SL Tel: (0580) 211044
Kent County Council	Countryside Group, Planning Department, Springfield, Maidstone, Kent ME14 2LX Tel: (0622) 696185
	Public Rights of Way Unit, Highways Dept, Astley House, Hastings Road, Maidstone, Kent ME15 7SQ Tel: (0622) 696921
	Public Transport Information Tel: (0800) 696996
Kent Trust for Nature Conservation	Tyland Barn, Sandling, Maidstone, Kent ME14 3BD Tel: (0622) 662012
Kentish Stour Countryside Project	Countryside Management Centre, Coldharbour Farm, Wye, Ashford, Kent TN25 5DB Tel: (0233) 813307
Long Distance Walkers' Association	Ann Sayer, 29 Twickenham Road, Teddington, Middlesex TW11 8AQ
National Trust	HQ, 36 Queen Anne's Gate, London SW1H 9AS Tel: (071) 222 9251
	Regional Office (Kent & Sussex), Scotney Castle, Lamberhurst, Tunbridge Wells, Kent TN3 8IN Tel: (0892) 890651

	Regional Office (Surrey), Polesden Lacey, Dorking, Surrey RH5 6BD Tel: (0372) 53401
North Downs Society	Mr M Nightingale, Wormshill Court, Wormshill, Sittingbourne, Kent ME9 0TS
North West Kent Countryside Project	Countryside Project Centre, Mead Crsecent, Dartford, Kent DA1 2SH Tel: (0322) 294727
Ramblers' Assocaition	HQ, 1/5 Wandsworth Road, London SW8 2XX Tel: (071) 582 6878
	Area Secretary, 42 Waldron Drive, Loose, Maidstone, Kent ME15 9TH Tel: (0622) 744207
Royal Society for Nature Conservation	The Green, Witham Park, Waterside South, Lincoln LN5 7RJ Tel: (0522) 544400
Royal Society for the Protection of Birds	HQ, The Lodge, Sandy, Beds SG19 2PL Tel: (0767) 680551
	SE England Office, 8 Church Street, Shoreham-by-Sea, West Sussex BN4 5DQ Tel: (0273) 463642
Sports Council	PO Box 480, National Sports Centre, Ledrington Road, London SE19 2BQ Tel: (081) 778 8600
Surrey County Council	Rights of Way Unit, Highways Department, County Hall, Kingston-upon-Thames, KT1 2DN Tel: (081) 541 8800
	Countryside Management Division, Planning Department, West House, Merrow Lane, Guildford, Surrey GU4 7BQ Tel: (0483) 517597 or 541595

Surrey Wildlife Trust	School Lane, Pirbright, Woking, Surrey GU24 0JN Tel: (0483) 488055
Trail Riders Fellowship	34 Oak Road, Barton-under-Needwood, Burton-on-Trent, Staffs DE13 8LR
White Cliffs Countryside Project	6 Cambridge Terrace, Dover, Kent CT16 1JT Tel: (0304) 241806

BUS SERVICES

Changes occur regularly in the companies providing bus services which either cross the North Downs Way or serve the towns and villages nearby. In order to prevent the information in this guide becoming out of date very quickly, the Facilities and Accommodation section identifies the route numbers rather than the names of the operating companies. Having obtained this information from the guide you should then contact either Surrey or Kent County Councils for further details, including times. Both Councils produce a selection of booklets detailing services in different parts of the two counties and these are updated regularly.

Passenger Transport Group Highways & Transportation Dept Surrey County Council Room 311 County Hall Kingston-upon-Thames Surrey KT1 2DN	Public Transport Section Highways & Transportation Dept Kent County Council Springfield Maidstone Kent ME14 2LR
Tel: (081) 541 8800	Tel: 0800 696996

RAIL SERVICES

There are many railway stations close to the North Downs Way, and it is often possible to walk sections of the route in one direction with a return by train to your starting point. For details of the services please contact one of the following numbers:

General enquiries:	Surrey	0256 464966
	Kent	0732 770111
24 hours:	both counties	071 834 2345

FACILITIES AND ACCOMMODATION

We have divided the route of the North Downs Way into 13 maps at a scale of approximately 1:50,000. The map run from West to East with towns and villages listed alongside. Each place is followed by a four figure grid reference, distance from the North Downs Way and the facilities available. In some cases all the facilities may not be at the same distance from the National Trail; where accommodation is concerned you may wish to find out the distance in advance, if this is not clear from the entry in the guide. Prices are per person for bed and breakfast, unless otherwise stated. The prices are for guidance only and should be confirmed with the establishment in question.

As mentioned elsewhere, bus route numbers are identified where possible. The maps give some indication of bus routes which cross the North Downs Way.

Key to facilites:	
S	Single Room
D	Double Room
T	Twin Room
F	Family Room
EM	Evening Meal
PL	Packed Lunch
Tel	Telephone
PO	Post Office
Rest	Restaurant

KEY TO MAPS

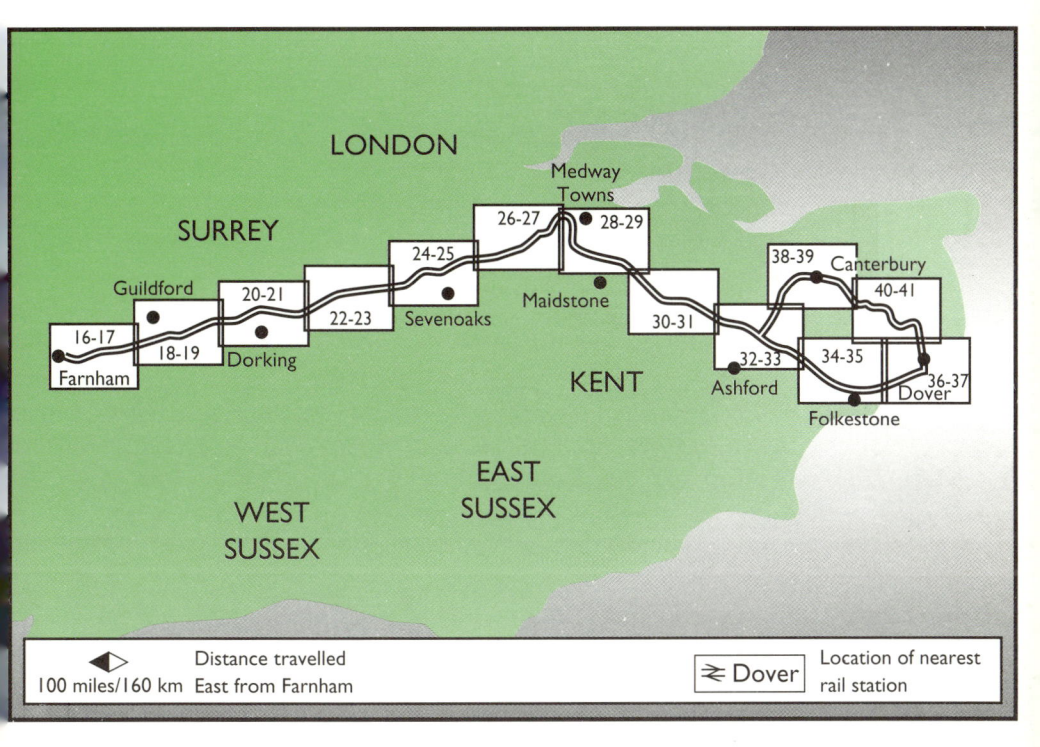

Bluebells

Mrs A Crawford, High Wray, 73 Lodge Hill Road, Farnham GU10 3RB
Tel: (0252) 715589
S2, £16; D1, £20; T2, £20; EM, PL by arr; dogs by arr. Also studio sleeps 2/3 in 3 acre garden.

Bishops Table Hotel, 27 West Street, Farnham GU9 7DR
Tel: (0252) 715545/710222
S8; D8; T2; Single £70, Double £85 per room; EM; no dogs
Closed 23 Dec-4 Jan. All rooms individually decorated.

FARNHAM (SU8446)
Start/End of North Downs Way
Range of facilities; Railway Station; Bus Services

THE SANDS (SU8846)
0.25 mile/0.4 km south
PO/Gen Store; Tel; Pub: The Barley Mow
Restricted bus service (515, 545, 565)

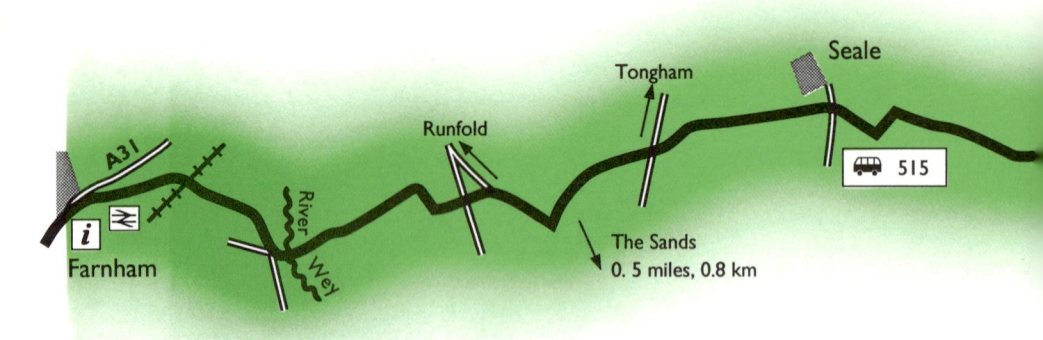

Near Puttenham

Near Compton

PAGE 16

Wanborough
2 miles, 3.25 km

B3000

565

Puttenham

A3(T)

290 448

Compton
0.5 miles, 0.8 km

SEALE (SU8947)
On North Downs Way
Rest/Tearooms; Tel; Restricted bus service (515, 545, 565)

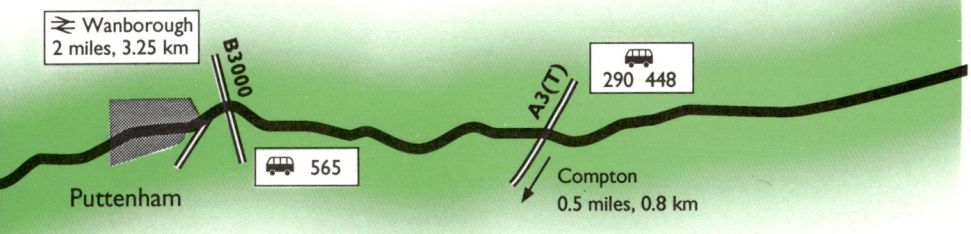

PUTTENHAM (SU9347)
On North Downs Way
PO/Gen Store; Tel; Pub: The Good Intent; Rest: Jolly Farmer (0.5 mile/0.8km S of NDW) Restricted bus service (545, 565)

COMPTON (SU9547)
0.5 mile/0.8km south
Tel; Pub: The Harrow Inn; Tea shop on NDW (Watts Gallery); Bus services (290, 448)

ST CATHERINES (SU9847)
On North Downs Way
Tel; Pub: The Ship

GUILDFORD (SU9949)
Town Centre 1 mile/1.6km north
Range of facilities; Railway Station; Bus Services

Mrs M Bourne, Weybrook House, 113 Stoke Road, Guildford GU1 1ET
Tel: (0483) 302394
S1, £20; D1, £16; F1, negotiable; PL; dogs by arr.

Mrs L Atkinson, Atkinsons Guest House, 129 Stoke Road, Guildford GU1 1ET
Tel: (0483) 38260
S1, £20; D1, £35; T1, £39; F1, £50; (all prices per room); room service; PL; no dogs.

Greyfriars, 9 Castle Hill, Guildford GU1 3SX
Tel: (0483) 61795
S2; T1; F or D1; £13-£14. PL by arr; no dogs.

Mrs J Braithwaite, 'Hillcote', 11 Castle Hill, Guildford GU1 3SX
Tel: (0483) 63324
S1, £14; T2, £13. EM, PL by arr; no dogs.

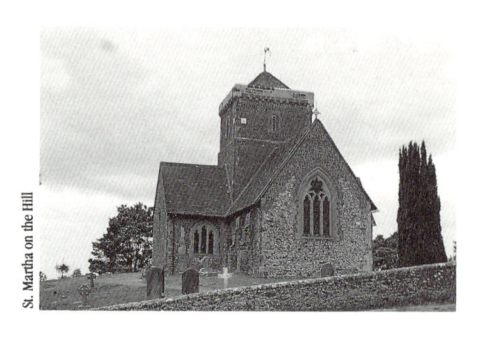

St. Martha on the Hill

CHILWORTH
1 mile/1.6km south
Pub: The Percy Arms; Railway Station

NEWLANDS CORNER (TQ0449)
On North Downs Way
Car Park; Toilets; Info Centre; Cafe; Tel
Restricted bus services (25, 433, 448, 588)

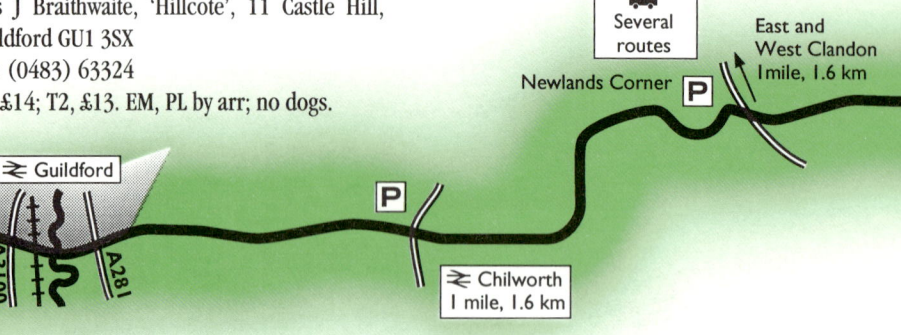

Beevers Farm, Chinthurst Lane, Bramley, Guildford GU5 0DR
Tel: (0483) 898764
T1, £13-£15; F1, £13-£15 (half price under 12), 1 treble en-suite room, £18.50 pp. Dogs by arr; closed Xmas-end Feb.

GODALMING
2 miles/3km south
Meads Hotel, 65 Mead Row, Godalming GU7 3HS
Tel: (0483) 421800
S, £23; D, £35; T, £35; F, £45; (prices per room); PL by arr; dogs by arr.

EAST AND WEST CLANDON (TQ0551)
2 miles/3km north
Pubs: The Bulls Head (W Clandon); The Queen's Head (E Clandon); Tel; Bus Services (408, 432, 433, 479)

Mr & Mrs C G F Hughes, Ways Cottage, Lime Grove, West Clandon GU4 7UT
S, £15; D or T, £18.50 per person or £30 for 2. Transport to and from NDW by arr.

SHERE (TQ 0747)
1 mile/1.6km south
Shops; PO; Rest/Cafe; Lloyds Bank; Tel; Pubs:
The Prince of Wales; The White Horse
Bus Services (21, 22, 25, 525, 573, 588)

Mrs M James, Manor Cottage, Shere, Guildford
GU5 9JE
Tel: (0483) 202979
S1; D1; EM; PL; no dogs, no smokers; open Apr-Oct inc.

GOMSHALL (TQ0847)
1 mile/1.6km south
PO/Gen Store; Rests; Tel; Pub: The Compasses Inn; Railway Station; Bus Services (22, 25, 525, 573)

DUNLEY HILL FARM (TQ1150)
1 mile/1.6km north
Pub: The Ranmore Arms; Tearooms: Old Cartlodge (seasonal)

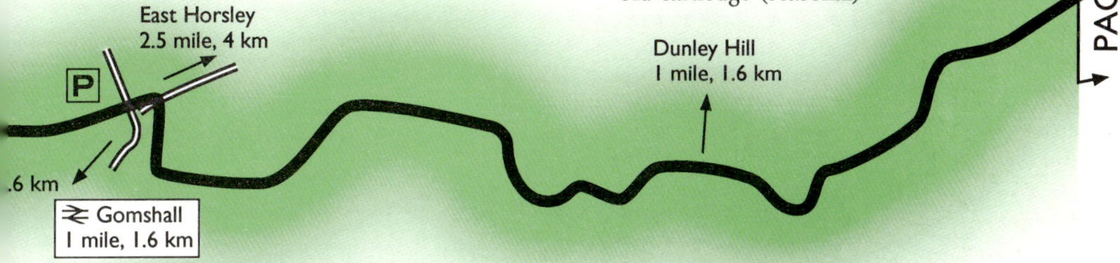

Near Gomshall

East Horsley
2.5 mile, 4 km

Dunley Hill
1 mile, 1.6 km

PAGE 18

.6 km

≷ Gomshall
1 mile, 1.6 km

Newlands Corner

17

WESTCOTT (TQ1448)

2 miles/3km south
Shops/PO; Pubs: The Cricketers; The Crown Inn; Prince of Wales Hotel; Tel: Bus Services

Mr & Mrs Nyman, Corner House, Guildford Road, Westcott, nr Dorking RH4 3QE
Tel: (0306) 888798
S, £15; D/T, £30; F, £45; (prices per room); PL by arr; dogs by arr.

DORKING (TQ1649)

1 mile/1.6 mile south
Range of facilities; Railway Stations; Bus Services (several operators)

Westward House, Westcott Road, Dorking RH4 3EA
Tel: (0306) 887700
S1, £20; D1, £17; T1, £17; F1 by arr; PL by arr; dogs by arr.

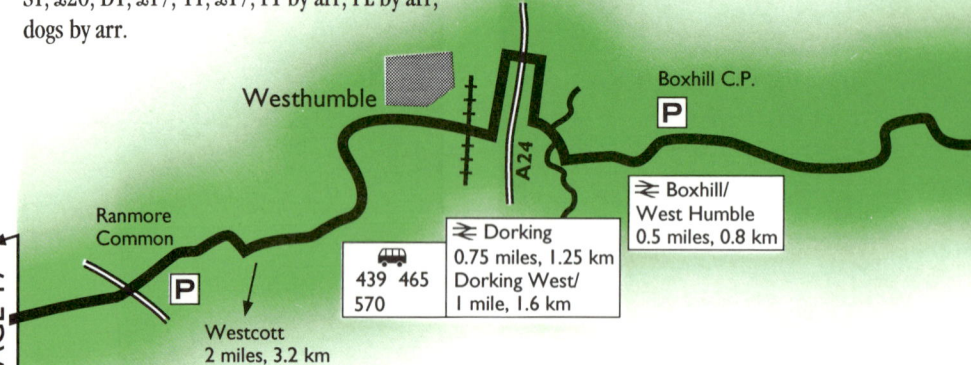

Mrs M Walton, The Waltons, 5 Rose Hill, Dorking RH4 2EG
Tel: (0306) 883127
D1, T1, F1, £15-£20 per person; EM, PL by arr; dogs by arr; pay phone; tea/coffee available.

WEST HUMBLE (TQ1651)

0.5 mile/0.8km north
Pub: The Stepping Stones; Pub/Rest: The Burford Bridge; Tel; Railway Station (Boxhill and West Humble); Bus Services (439, 465, 570)

Pyramidal Orchid

Mrs M Chisman, Old House Cottage, Mickleham, Dorking RH5 6EH
Tel: (0372) 375050
S, £18; D, £30; (prices per room); T, £30; EM, PL by arr; dogs by arr; transport to/from station or Dorking by arr.

BOXHILL COUNTRY PARK (TQ1951)

On North Downs Way
National Trust info. centre with refreshments; car park/toilets

BOXHILL (TQ1951)
0.5 mile/0.8km north
PO; Newsagent/Gen Store; other shops; Pub: Hand in Hand; Rest: La Collina; Railway Station at Boxworth (1 mile/1.6km south); Bus Services (516, 520, 551)

PEBBLE COOMBE (TQ2153)
1 mile/1.6km north
Tel

BUCKLAND (TQ2250)
1 mile/1.6km south
PO/Gen Store; Tel; Pub: The Jolly Farmer; Railway Station at Betchworth; Bus Service (573)

MOGADOR (TQ2453)
0.5 mile/0.8km north
Pub: The Sportsman

LOWER KINGWOOD (TQ2453)
1 mile/1.6km north
Pub: The Fox; PO; Shops; Tel; Bus Services (406, 420, 422, 520, 522, 727)

REIGATE (TQ2550)
1 mile/1.6km south
Range of facilities; Railway Station, Bus Services (several operators)

REIGATE HILL (TQ2552)
On North Downs Way
Car Park/Toilets; Refreshment Bar; Pub: The Yew Tree (0.5 mile/0.8km south)

Box Hill

REDHILL (TQ2850)
2 miles/3km south
Range of facilities; Railway Station; Bus Services (several operators)

MERSTHAM (TQ2953)
0.5 mile/0.8km south
PO; Tel; Shops; Pubs: Railway Arms, The Iron Horse, The Inn on the Pond, The Griffin; Railway Station; Bus Services (304, 405)

GRAVELLEY HILL (TQ3353)
On North Downs Way
Car Parking (limited)

CATERHAM (TQ3455)
1 mile/1.6km north
Range of facilities; Railway Station; Bus Services (302, 409, 411)

GODSTONE (TQ3551)
2 miles/3km south
Range of facilities

Godstone Hotel, The Green, Godstone RH9 8DT
Tel: (0883) 742461
S, £25; D5, £35; T2, £35; F1, £45; (prices per room); EM; PL by arr; dogs by arr; all rooms ensuite; tea/coffee facilities

SOUTH HAWKE (TQ3754)
On North Downs Way
Car parking

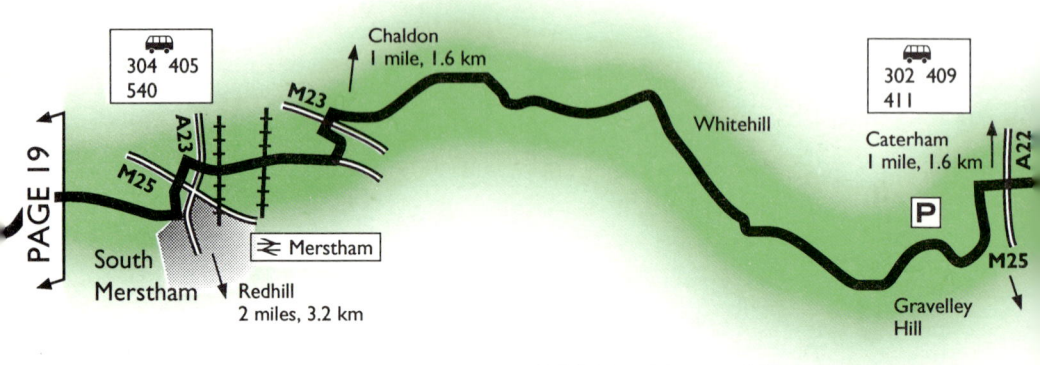

River Mole

CHALDON (TQ3155)
1 mile/1.6km north
Tel; Restricted bus service (540)

WHITEHILL (TQ3253)
On North Downs Way
Pub: The Harrow

OXTED/LIMPSFIELD (TQ3952)
1 mile/2km south
Range of facilities; Railway Station; Bus Services (several operators)
Jenny Snell, Rosehaven, 12 Hoskins Road, Oxted RH8 9HT
Tel: (0883) 712700
S1, T2; PL by arr; no dogs; closed Oct-Dec.

20

St. Katharine, Merstham

Mrs M F Mills, Old Forge House, Merle Common,
Oxted RH8 0JB
Tel: (0883) 715969
S1, D1, T1, £16 per person; PL by arr; dogs by arr; transport available to/from Oxted/Limpsfield; closed Xmas/New Year.

BOTLEY HILL (TQ3955)
On North Downs Way
Tel

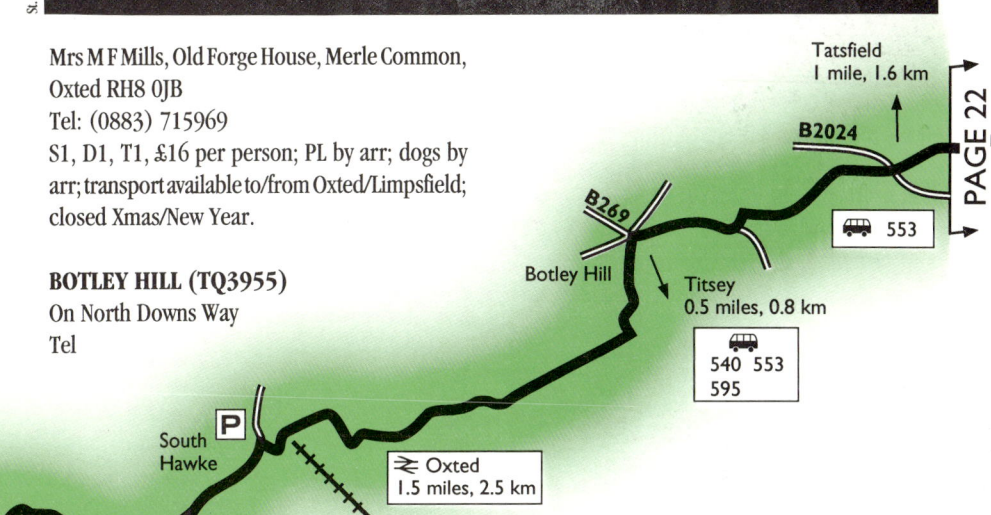

TITSEY (TQ4055)
0.5 mile/0.8km south
Tel; Bus Services (540, 553, 595)

TATSFIELD (TQ4157)
1 mile/1.6km north
PO/Gen Store; Fruit & Veg Shop; Tel; Pub: The Old Ship; Bus Services (several operators)

Churchill statue, Westerham

WESTERHAM (TQ4554)
2 miles/3km south
Wide range of shops; PO; cafés/Restaurants; Banks/Building Societies;
Tel; Car Parks, Toilets; Bus Services (320, 410, 420, 425, 483,553)

HAWLEY'S CORNER (TQ4356)
1 mile/1.6km north
Pub/Rest: The Spinning Wheel; Tel.

KNOCKHOLT (TQ4859)
0.5 mile/0.8km north
Newsagent/confectioner; Pubs: The Tally Ho!, The Crown, The Three Horseshoes, The Harrow Inn; Tel. Bus Service (R5)

BRASTED (TQ4755)
2 miles/3km south
PO/Gen Store; Newsagent/Confectioner; Tel. Pubs: The White Hart, The Kings Arms, The Bull Inn, Stanhope Arms, Bus Services (238, 420, 425, 483)

SUNDRIDGE (TQ4955)
3 miles/4.75km south
PO/Gen Store; Pubs: The White Horse; The Lamb; Bus Services (238, 420, 425, 483)

DUNTON GREEN (TQ5157)
1.5 miles/2.4km south
Several Shops; Tel; Pubs: The Rose and Crown (on NDW), The Duke's Head; The Miner's Arms; Railway Station; Bus Services (402, 431, 432)

Donnington Manor, London Road, Dunton Green, Sevenoaks
Tel (0732) 462681
D34, T26, F3. EM; PL by arr; dogs by arr.

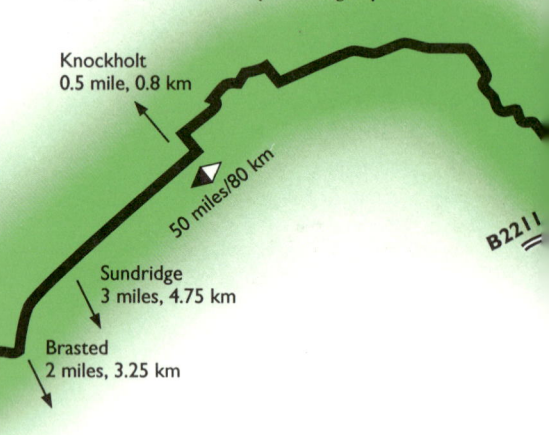

Mrs C Morris, Chaddesden, Morants Court Road, Dunton Green, Sevenoaks
Tel (0732) 462868
S £18; D £16; T £16; PL by arr; dogs by arr; Pubs/Rest walking dist.

RIVERHEAD (TQ5156)
2 miles/3km south
Northern suburb of Sevenoaks; range of facilities; Railway Station; Bus Services (402, 406, 431, 432)

Mrs N T Godsal, The Orchard House, Brasted Chart, Westerham, Kent TN16 1LR
Tel: (0959) 563702
S1, £16; T2, £15; EM, PL by arr; no dogs; closed Christmas & New Year

OTFORD (TQ5259)

On North Downs Way

PO; Chemist; range of shops; Lloyds Bank (11-2 Mon - Fri);

Pubs: The Horns; The Bull; The Crown; The Woodman; The Rising Sun (Twitton); Railway Station; Bus Services (321, 431, 432, 434)

Moat Bungalow, Station Road, Otford, Sevenoaks TN14 5QU
Tel: (0959) 524165
S1, £14; T1, £28 (room); EM by arr; dogs by arr.

Mrs C M Hord, 24A Pilgrims Way East, Otford, Sevenoaks, TN14 5QN
Tel: (0959) 523743; Fax: (0959) 525287
S £18; T £18; EM, PL by arr; no dogs; now open all year; no smoking

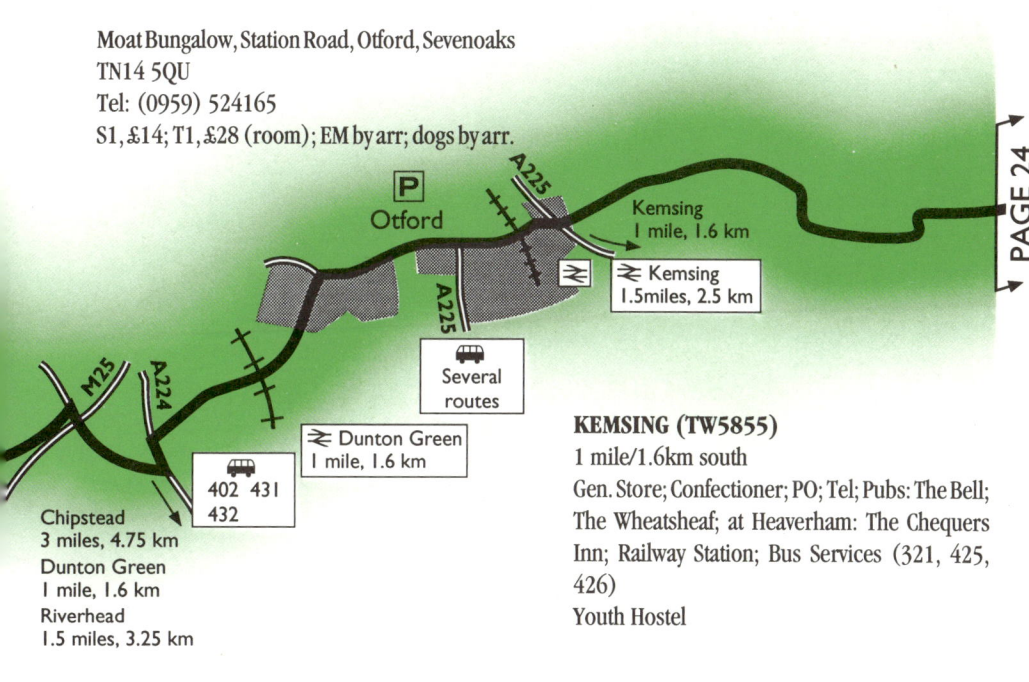

KEMSING (TW5855)

1 mile/1.6km south

Gen. Store; Confectioner; PO; Tel; Pubs: The Bell; The Wheatsheaf; at Heaverham: The Chequers Inn; Railway Station; Bus Services (321, 425, 426)

Youth Hostel

Bishops Palace, Otford

BOROUGH GREEN (TQ6057)
2 miles/3km south
Range of facilities; Railway Station (Borough Green & Wrotham); Bus Services (70, 222, 306, 406)

Mrs B R Oxley, Stone Ridge, 168 Maidstone Road, Borough Green, Sevenoaks
TN15 8JD

Speckled Wood

Tel: (0732) 882053
S1 £22; D1 £18 p.p.; T1 £18 p.p.; EM, PL by arr; no dogs; drying facilities

WROTHAM (TQ6159)
0.5 mile/0.8km south
Several shops; PO; Nat West Bank; Car Park; Tel; Pubs: The Rose & Crown; George & Dragon; Three Post Boys; The Bull;
Bus Services (306)

C & J Thomas, Hillside House, Gravesend Road, Wrotham TN15 7JH
Tel: (0732) 822564
S £15; D £30 (£16 p.p.); T £32; EM by arr; PL by arr; dogs by arr;
closed Xmas and New Year

The Bull Hotel, Bull Lane, Wrotham TN15 7RF
Tel: (0732) 885522/883092; Fax: (0732) 886288
S1 £40; D3 £25 p.p.; T5 £20 p.p.; F £15 p.p.; EM, PL; dogs by arr.

Mrs D Jolliffe, Green Hill House, High Street, Wrotham TN15 7AH
Tel: (0732) 883069
S £20; T £32 per room; D £32 per room; PL by arr; no smoking

TROTTISCLIFFE (TQ6460)
1 mile/1.6km south
Tel; Pubs: The George, The Plough; Bus Services (58)

VIGO (TQ6361)
On the North Downs Way
Farm Shop; Pub: The Vigo; Trosley Country Park (Car Park, Toilets); Bus Services (306, 308, Post bus)

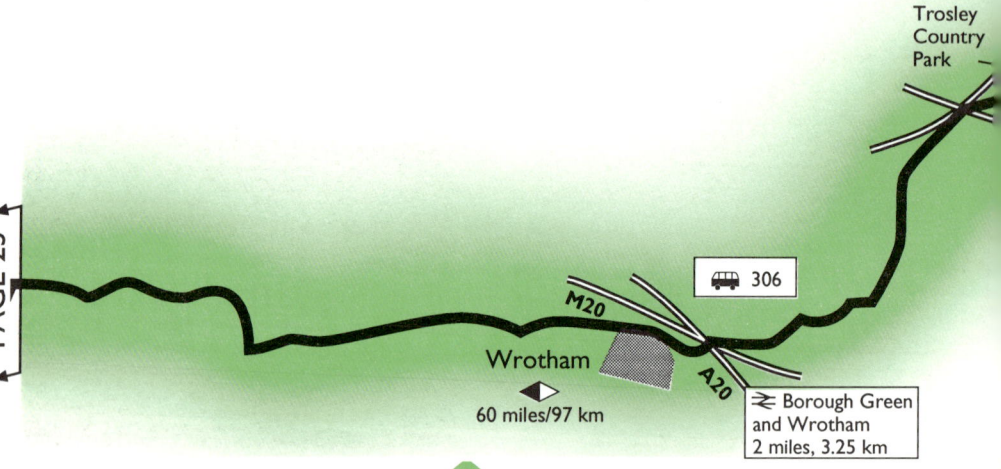

RYARSH (TQ6760)
2 miles/3km south
PO/Gen. Store; Tel; Pub: The Duke of Wellington;
Bus Service (58)

Mrs J Edwards, Heavers Farm, Ryarsh, West
Malling ME19 5JU
Tel: (0732) 842074
D1, T2, from £15; EM, PL by arr; dogs by arr;
closed Xmas and New Year

BIRLING (TQ6860)
2 miles/3km south
Pub: The Nevill Bull; Bus Service (58)

UPPER HALLING (TQ6964)
0.5 mile/0.8km east
Pubs: The Pilgrim's Rest, The Black Boy; Tel.
Bus Service (151)

PAGE 26

Halling
1.5 miles, 2.5 km

≷ Halling
1.5 miles, 2.5 km

Upper Halling
2 miles, 3.25 km

Birling
2 miles, 3.25 km

Vigo Village

Ryarsh
2 miles, 3.25 km

Trottiscliffe
1 mile, 1.6 km

Above Halling

HALLING (TQ7064)
1 mile/2km east
PO/Gen. Store; Confectioner/Newsagent; Tel;
Pubs: The Plough; The New Bell Inn; Homeward
Bound;
Railway Station; Bus Service (151)

25

PAGE 25

A228

River Medway

69 miles/111 km
Medway Towns
1.5 miles, 2.5 km

Cuxton

Wouldham
1 mile, 1.6 km

Burham
1 mile, 1.6 km

M2

Rochester
2 miles, 3.25 km

A229

Blue Bell Hill
Picnic Site P

Medway Towns
2 miles, 3.25 km
Blue Bell Hill
0.5 miles, 0.8 km

A229

Boxley
1 mile, 1.6 km

CUXTON (TQ7167)
1 mile/1.6km south
PO; General Store; Tel;
Pub: The White Hart;
Railway Station; Bus
Service (151)

MEDWAY TOWNS
Chatham, Gillingham,
Rochester
Wide range of facilities;
Railway Stations and Bus
Services

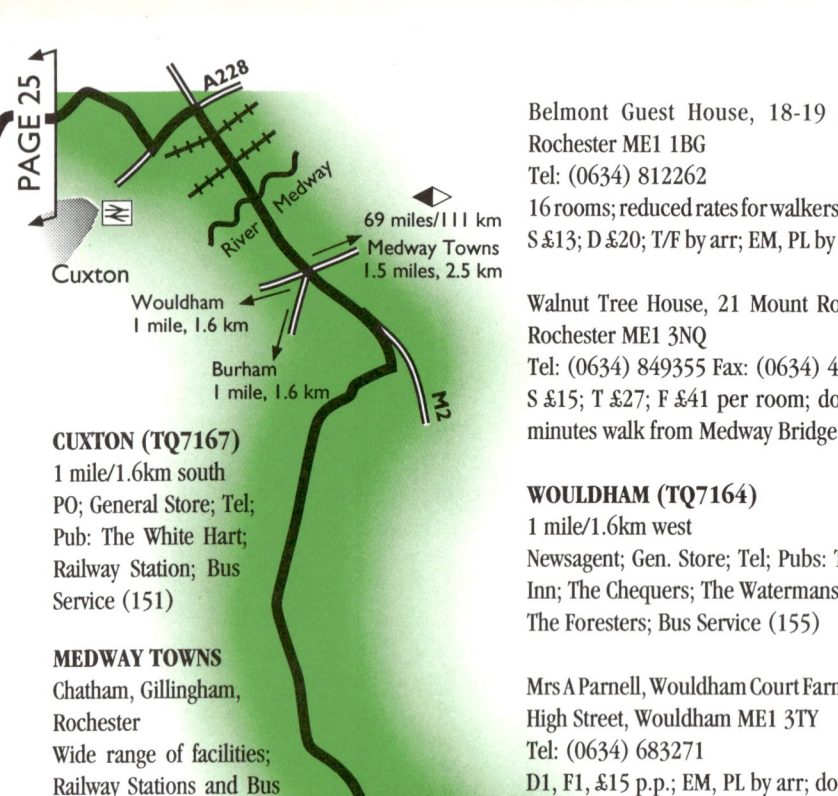

Mrs S Beggs, St Ouen, 98 Borstal
Road, Rochester ME1 3BD
Tel: (0634) 843528
S1 £16; D1 £16; T1 £16; PL; dogs
by arr.

Mrs S Field, Condor House, The Street, Bredhurst,
Gillingham ME7 3JY
Tel: (0634) 232988
S1 £17-50; T3 £30 per room; PL by arr; dogs
accepted; swimming pool

Belmont Guest House, 18-19 New Road,
Rochester ME1 1BG
Tel: (0634) 812262
16 rooms; reduced rates for walkers and cyclists:
S £13; D £20; T/F by arr; EM, PL by arr; no dogs

Walnut Tree House, 21 Mount Road, Borstal,
Rochester ME1 3NQ
Tel: (0634) 849355 Fax: (0634) 402730
S £15; T £27; F £41 per room; dogs by arr; 5
minutes walk from Medway Bridge

WOULDHAM (TQ7164)
1 mile/1.6km west
Newsagent; Gen. Store; Tel; Pubs: The Medway
Inn; The Chequers; The Watermans Arms; Rest:
The Foresters; Bus Service (155)

Mrs A Parnell, Wouldham Court Farmhouse, 246
High Street, Wouldham ME1 3TY
Tel: (0634) 683271
D1, F1, £15 p.p.; EM, PL by arr; dogs by arr.

BURHAM (TQ7362)
1 mile/1.6km south west
PO/Gen. Store; Grocer; Baker; Newsagent; Tel;
Pubs/Rest: The Windmill, The Toastmasters, The
Golden Eagle, The Fleur de Lis.
Bus Service (155)

Bee Orchid

26

Kits Coty House

BLUE BELL HILL (TQ7462)
0.5 mile/0.8km east
PO/Gen Store; Tel; Pubs: Robin Hood, Upper Bell Inn; Lower Bell Inn; Picnic site on NDW with car park (no toilets); Bus Services (101, 126, 142, 150)

BOXLEY (TQ7759)
1 mile/1.6km south
Rest (Boxley House Hotel); Pub: The King's Arms; Tel; Bus Service (130)

Boxley House Hotel, Boxley, Maidstone ME14 3DZ
Tel: (0622) 692269
S5 £40; D7 £55; T4 £55; F2; EM, PL; dogs by arr.

Mr & Mrs J Munson, Barn Cottage, Harbourland, Boxley, Maidstone ME14 3DN
Tel: (0622) 675891
T3 £15; EM, PL; no dogs; closed Xmas; no smoking

DETLING (TQ7958)
0.5 mile/0.8km south
PO/Gen. Store; Pub: The Cock Horse; Tel; Bus Services (333, 341, Post bus)

THURNHAM (TQ8058)
0.5 mile/0.8km south
Pub: The Black Horse; Cobham Manor (car park, coffee shop, circular walks, info. Tel (0622) 738497/738871)

Detling
79 miles/127 km

PAGE 28

Hucking
1 mile, 1.6 km

Mrs B Gibbs, Toadflax Cottage, Pilgrims Way, Hollingbourne, Maidstone ME17 1UT
Tel: (0622) 880652
D1 £35; (£20 single); no dogs; no smoking; closed Nov - Jan.

Hollingbourne

≷ Hollingbourne
1.5 miles, 2.5 km

HUCKING (TQ8458)
1 mile/1.6km north
Pub: The Hook and Hatchet

HOLLINGBOURNE (TQ8455)
1 mile/1.6km south
PO; Newsagent/Confectioner; Pubs: The Dirty Habit (on NDW); The Sugar Loaves; The Windmill; Railway Station; Bus Services (12B)

Mrs F Leer, Manorfield, Pilgrims Way, Hollingbourne, Maidstone ME17 1RD
Tel: (0622) 880373
T1 £32; F1 £40; (prices per room); EM, PL by arr; no dogs; closed 20 Dec - 20 Jan; open air swimming pool

Philip & Shania Reed, The Limes, 53 Eyhorne Street, Hollingbourne, Maidstone ME17 1TS
Tel: (0622) 880554
S1 £16; T1 £16; PL by arr; no dogs; closed Dec - Jan.

Harrietsham
1 mile, 1.6 km

≷ Harrietsham
1 mile, 1.6 km

Archbishops Palace, Charing

Woodhouses, 49 Eyhorne Street, Hollingbourne, Maidstone ME17 1TR
Tel: (0622) 880594
£16 p.p. B & B; 3 T/D; all en-suite; teamaking facilities; EM, PL

Mrs D Passey, Westmead, West Street, Harrietsham, Maidstone ME17 1SD
Tel: (0622) 859448
D1; T/F1; £15 per person; PL by arr. no dogs; closed Xmas

92 miles/148 km

Lenham
1 mile, 1.6 km

≷ Lenham
1 mile, 1.6 km

HARRIETSHAM (TQ8652)
1 mile/1.6km south
PO; Grocery; Newsagent; Pubs: The Bank House; The Roe Buck; The Bell; Restaurant (on A20); Tel; Railway Station; Bus Services (10, Post bus)

Mrs H Atkins, Mannamead, Pilgrims Way, Harrietsham, Maidstone ME17 1BT
Tel: (0622) 859336
S1 £16-£18; D1 £17 (en-suite); T1 £15; no dogs; closed mid Dec - mid Jan.

LENHAM (TQ8952)
1 mile/1.6km south
Range of shops; PO; Nat West Bank; 2 Restaurants; Pubs: The Dog and Bear, The Red Lion; Car Park; Toilets; Tel; Railway Station; Bus Services (10, Post bus)

PAGE 30 →

29

CHARING (TQ9549)

0.5 mile/0.8km south

Range of shops; PO; Nat West Bank; Restaurants; Pubs: The King's Head, The Royal Oak, The Queen's Head; Car Park; Tel; Railway Station; Bus Services (10, 519, 669)

◀ PAGE 29

519 669

A252

Charing

≋ Wanborough
2 miles, 3.25 km

The Downs above Wye

Mrs R Bigwood, Armada House, 9 The High Street, Charing TN27 0HU
Tel: (0233) 712822
S1, D1, T1; PL by arr; no dogs; close to rests, pubs, shops,

Mrs S M Tucker, Peckwater House, 17 The High Street, Charing TN27 0HU
Tel: (0233) 712592
D2, T2, F1; £18-50 - £22-50 p.p.; PL by arr; no dogs; closed Xmas; close to rests, pubs, shops

Westwell
0.5 miles, 0.8 km

Wye from Wye Downs

30

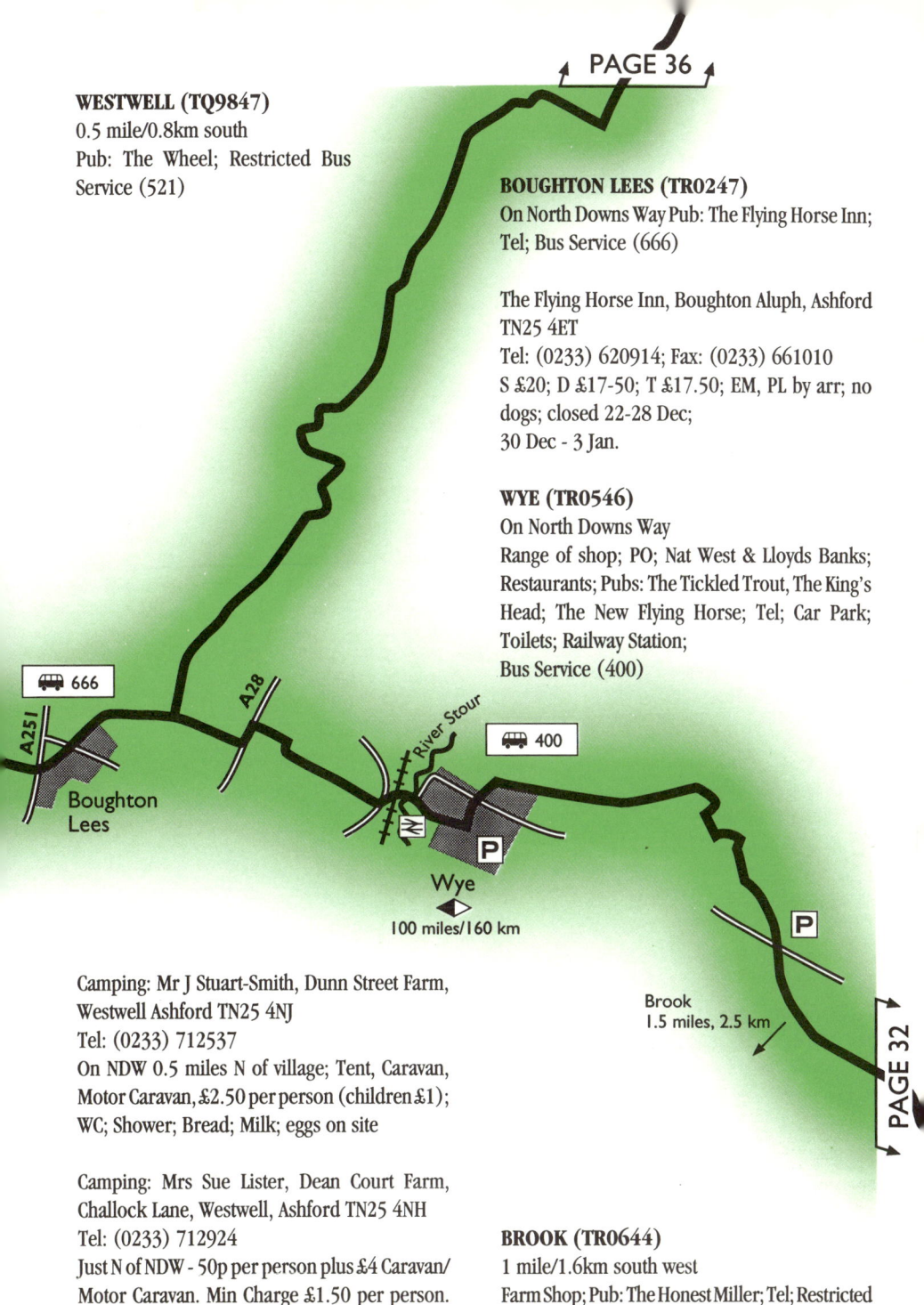

WESTWELL (TQ9847)
0.5 mile/0.8km south
Pub: The Wheel; Restricted Bus Service (521)

BOUGHTON LEES (TR0247)
On North Downs Way Pub: The Flying Horse Inn; Tel; Bus Service (666)

The Flying Horse Inn, Boughton Aluph, Ashford TN25 4ET
Tel: (0233) 620914; Fax: (0233) 661010
S £20; D £17-50; T £17.50; EM, PL by arr; no dogs; closed 22-28 Dec; 30 Dec - 3 Jan.

WYE (TR0546)
On North Downs Way
Range of shop; PO; Nat West & Lloyds Banks; Restaurants; Pubs: The Tickled Trout, The King's Head; The New Flying Horse; Tel; Car Park; Toilets; Railway Station;
Bus Service (400)

Wye
100 miles/160 km

Brook
1.5 miles, 2.5 km

Camping: Mr J Stuart-Smith, Dunn Street Farm, Westwell Ashford TN25 4NJ
Tel: (0233) 712537
On NDW 0.5 miles N of village; Tent, Caravan, Motor Caravan, £2.50 per person (children £1); WC; Shower; Bread; Milk; eggs on site

Camping: Mrs Sue Lister, Dean Court Farm, Challock Lane, Westwell, Ashford TN25 4NH
Tel: (0233) 712924
Just N of NDW - 50p per person plus £4 Caravan/Motor Caravan. Min Charge £1.50 per person. Dogs by arr; WC; Washing facilities

BROOK (TR0644)
1 mile/1.6km south west
Farm Shop; Pub: The Honest Miller; Tel; Restricted Bus Service (518)

HASTINGLEIGH (TR0945)
1 mile/1.6km north
PO/Gen. Store; Pub: The Bowl; Tel; Bus Services (620, 518)

Mrs J Denny, High Lodge, Elmsted, Nr Ashford TN25 5JH
Tel: (0233) 750234
S1, D1, F1; £16 p.p.; EM by arr (£8); PL; dogs accepted; no smoking; 1 mile/1.6km from NDW.

BRABOURNE (TR1041)
1 mile/1.6km south
Pub: The Five Bells; Tel; Bus Restricted Service (518)

STOWTING (TR1241)
On North Downs Way;
Pub: The Tiger Inn; Tel

Mrs C Cole, Water Farm, Stowting, Ashford TN25 6BA
Tel: (0303) 862401
T1 (en suite), D1; £16-50 p.p.; PL by arr; no dogs; no smoking; drying facilities

FARTHING COMMON (TR1340)
On North Downs Way
Car Parking

B M Wadie, Southfields, Farthing Common, Lyminge, Folkestone CT18 8DH
Tel: (0303) 862391
T2, £15 p.p.; EM, PL by arr; no dogs; closed Dec - Feb; on NDW.

POSTLING (TR1439)
0.5 mile/0.8km south
Tel

LYMINGE (TR1641)
1 mile/1.6km north
Range of shops; Nat West Bank; Pub: The Coach and Horses; Tel; Car Park/Toilets; Bus Services (17, 558, 559)

ETCHINGHILL (TR1639)
0.5 mile/0.8km north
Pub: The New Inn; Tel; Bus Service (17)

PADDLESWORTH (TR1939)
1 mile/1.6km north east
Pub: The Cat and Custard Pot

NEWINGTON (TR1839)
1 mile/1.6km south
Tel

Above Hastingleigh

Beachborough Park, Newington, Near Folkestone
CT18 8BW
Tel: (0303) 275432
S2, from £25; D4 from £35; T4 from £35; F2 from £60; EM, PL by arr; dogs by arr; licensed

FOLKESTONE (TR2236)
Town Centre 2 miles/3km south
Range of facilities; Railway Stations (Folkestone Central, F. West, F. Harbour);
Bus Services

Sheila and Paul Foot, Seacliffe, 3 Wear Bay Road, Folkestone CT19 6AT
Tel: (0303) 254592
S1; T1; F1; £13-£16 p.p.; EM, PL by arr; no dogs; no smoking

Mrs S Horton, Rob Roy Guest House, 227 Dover Road, Folkestone CT19 6NH
Tel: (0303) 253341
S £15-£18; D £25-£30; T £25-£30; F £32-£38; (prices per room); EM by arr; PL by arr; dogs by arr;

Mrs J Watts, Normandie Guest House, 39 Cheriton Road, Folkestone CT20 1DD
Tel: (0303) 256233
S1, D1, T2, F2; PL by arr; no dogs

Mr J M Donoghue, Abbey House Hotel, 5-6 Westbourne Gardens, (off Sandgate Road), Folkestone CT2 2JA
Tel: (0303) 255514
S3 £18; D2 £34; T5 £34; F4 £50; (prices per room); EM; PL by arr; dogs by arr.

Mrs E Page, Folke-Leas Guest House, 38 Cheriton Road, Folkestone CT20 1BZ
Tel: (0303) 251441
D2 £14; T2, £14; F2 £14; EM, PL by arr; dogs by arr.

Sunny Lodge Guest House, 85 Cheriton Road, Folkestone CT20 2QL
Tel: (0303) 251498
S2 £15; D2 £30; T2 £30; F2 £30+; (prices per room); PL by arr; no dogs; teamaking facilities; TVs.

Camping: Mr & Mrs Haddow, Black Horse Farm Caravan and Camping Park, 385 Canterbury Road, Densole, Folkestone CT18 7BG
Tel: (0303) 892665
3 miles/4.8km N of NDW; £1.50 per person (80p child 5 or under) plus £1.75 tent/caravan/motorcycle; £3.50 motor caravan; dogs by arr (60p); WC; Showers; laundry

111 miles/177 km
Etchinghill
🚌 17

Paddlesworth
1 mile, 1.6 km

Newington
1 mile, 1.6 km

Chandos Guest House, 77 Cheriton Road, Folkestone CT20 1DG
Tel: (0303) 851202
S5 £14; D2 £28; T1 £28; F2 £32; EM, PL by arr; dogs by arr.

Folkestone
2 miles, 3.25 km
≷ Folkestone
1.5 miles, 2.5 km

PAGE 34

Downland near Farthing Common

CAPEL-LE-FERNE (TR2538)
On North Downs Way
Pubs: The Valiant Sailor; The Royal Oak; Rest/Café: The White Cliffs Inn;
Bus Services (90, 93, 94)

DOVER (TR3142)
Start/end of North Downs Way
Wide range of facilities and accommodation; Railway Stations (Dover Priory, D. Western Docks); Bus Services

St Albans Guest House, 71 Folkestone Road, Dover CT17 9RZ
Tel: (0304) 206308
S1 £15; D4 £12-£15; T1 £12-£15; F2, £36 - £48 per room; no dogs; near Dover Priory Railway Station

Beaufort House Hotel, 17-20 East Cliff, Marine Parade, Dover CT16 1LU
Tel: (0304) 216444; Fax: (0304) 211100
S12 £22-£28; D12 £34-£42; T12 £34-£42; F9 £44-£59; (prices per room); EM, PL; dogs accepted; en-suite rooms; near Eastern Docks; licensed

Mr & Mrs C Oakley, Walletts Court, West Cliffe, St Margaret's, Dover CT15 6EW
Tel: (0304) 852424
S1 £30; D6, T2 £25-£30; F1 £70 for room; EM, PL by arr; no dogs; closed Xmas

L T Norton, Maison Dieu Guest House, 89 Maison Dieu Road, Dover CT16 1RU
Tel: (0304) 204033
S2, D1, T1, F3 £14; PL by arr; dogs by arr; closed Xmas

Mrs E Heynen, Chrislyn's Guest House, 15 Park Avenue, Dover CT16 1ES
Tel: (0304) 202302
S1 £15; D1 £30-£34; T2 £32-£36; F1 £40-£45; (prices per room); EM, PL by arr; no dogs

Canterbury Cathedral

Mr B M Bowes, Valjoy Guest House, 237 Folkestone Road, Dover CT17 9SL
Tel: (0304) 212160
S from £15; D from £28; T from £28; F from £35; (prices per room); EM, PL by arr; no dogs; closed Xmas Day/Boxing Day; tea/coffee facilities.

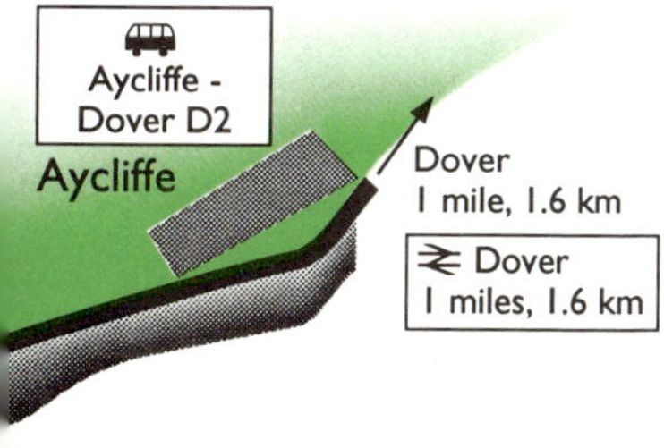

Mr & Mrs Roberts, Esther House, 55 Barton Road, Dover CT16 2NF
Tel: (0304) 241332
S1, T1, F1; EM by arr; PL; no dogs; no smoking; tea/coffee facilities, TVs.

A realignment of the route at Aycliffe is expected to occur during 1994. Please look out for the National Trail Waymarks.

Aycliffe - Dover D2

Aycliffe

Dover
1 mile, 1.6 km

Dover
1 miles, 1.6 km

Clifftops between Folkestone and Dover

CANTERBURY ROUTE

CHILHAM (TR0653)
On North Downs Way
PO; Pubs: The White Horse, The Woolpack Inn; Tel; Car Park/Toilets; Restaurant; Railway Station (1 mile/1.6km East of NDW); Bus Services (400, 519, 669)

The Woolpack Inn, High Street, Chilham, CT4 8DL
Tel: (0227) 730208
D5 £45; T3 £45; F3 £55; £35 per single occupancy; EM, PL by arr; dogs by arr.

Mrs P Hooker, Jullieberrie House, Canterbury Road, Chilham CT4 6DX
Tel: (0227) 730488
D2, T2; PL by arr; dogs by arr.

Mrs J Wood, Bagham Cross, Chilham CT4 8DU
Tel: (0227) 730264
D1, T1; £13-£14; PL by arr; no dogs; closed Nov - Easter

OLD WIVES LEES (TR0755)
On North Downs Way
PO/Gen. Store; Pub: The Star Inn; Tel; Bus Service (669)

CHARTHAM HATCH (TR1056)
On North Downs Way
Gen. Store; Pub: The Charter Arms; Tel; Picnic area on NDW (no toilets); Railway Station at Chartham (1 mile/1.6km south); Bus Service (669)

CANTERBURY (TR1557)
City with wide range of facilities and accommodation; Railway Stations, (Canterbury East, Canterbury West) and Bus Services

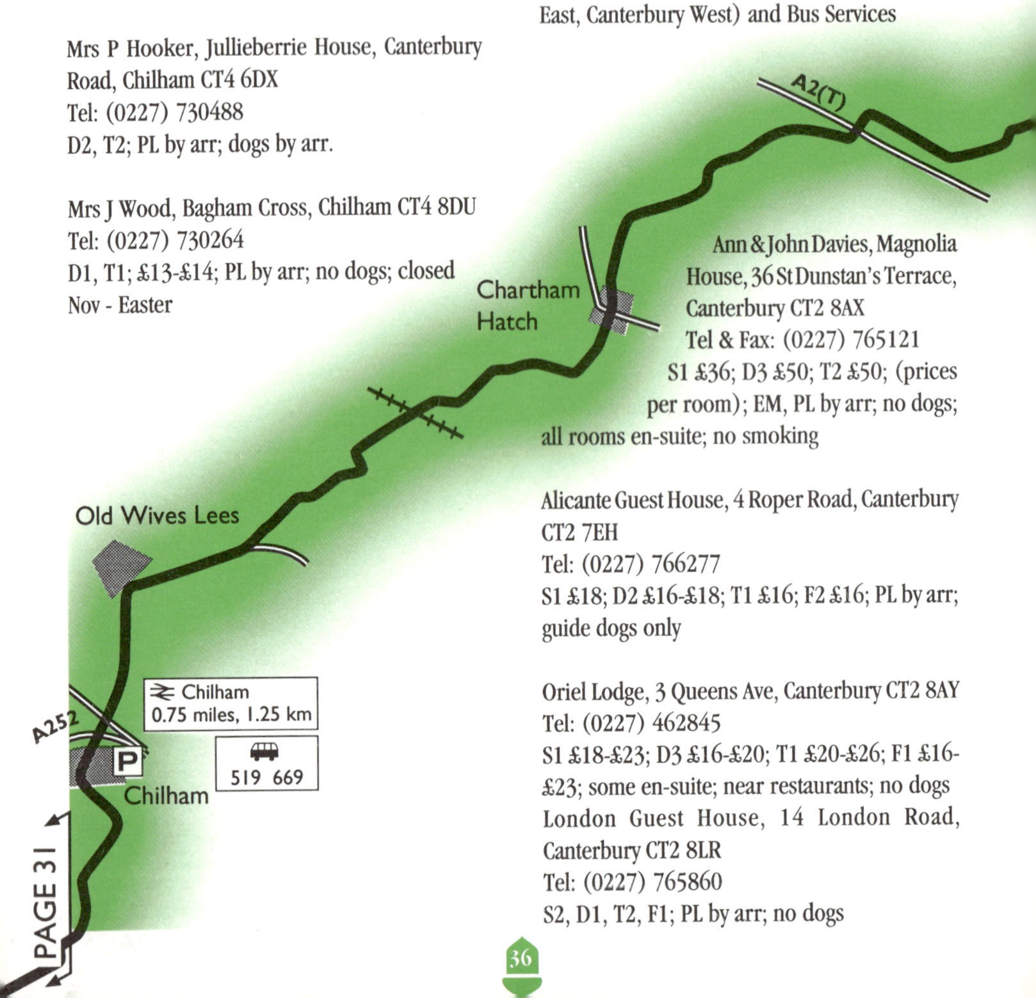

Ann & John Davies, Magnolia House, 36 St Dunstan's Terrace, Canterbury CT2 8AX
Tel & Fax: (0227) 765121
S1 £36; D3 £50; T2 £50; (prices per room); EM, PL by arr; no dogs; all rooms en-suite; no smoking

Alicante Guest House, 4 Roper Road, Canterbury CT2 7EH
Tel: (0227) 766277
S1 £18; D2 £16-£18; T1 £16; F2 £16; PL by arr; guide dogs only

Oriel Lodge, 3 Queens Ave, Canterbury CT2 8AY
Tel: (0227) 462845
S1 £18-£23; D3 £16-£20; T1 £20-£26; F1 £16-£23; some en-suite; near restaurants; no dogs

London Guest House, 14 London Road, Canterbury CT2 8LR
Tel: (0227) 765860
S2, D1, T2, F1; PL by arr; no dogs

Courtney Guest House, 4 London Road, Canterbury CT2 8LR
Tel: (0227) 769668
S1, D2, T1, F2; £12-£18; no dogs

Mrs J Wright, Milton House, 9 South Canterbury Road, Canterbury CT1 3LH
Tel: (0227) 765531
D1, T1; £14-£16; dogs by arr; closed Xmas

The Canterbury Hotel, 71 New Dover Road, Canterbury CT1 3DZ
Tel: (0227) 450551
S5 £40; D7 £50; T13 £50; F2 £60; EM, PL by arr; dogs accepted

Maynard Cottage, 106 Wincheap, Canterbury CT1 3RS
Tel: (0227) 454991 or (0850) 315558
S £20-£35; D £30-£42; T £30-£42; F £42-£52; EM, PL; dogs accepted; no smoking in bedrooms, Discount for stays of 2 nights+

BEKESBOURNE HILL (TR1956)
0.5 mile/0.8km north
Pub: The Unicorn; Railway Station

BEKESBOURNE (TR1955)
0.5 mile/0.8km north
Tel

BRIDGE (TR1854)
1 mile/1.6km south
PO; Gen/Food Stores; Newsagents; Pubs: The White Horse, The Plough and Harrow, The Red Lion; Restaurants; Tel; Bus Services (15, 15A, 16, 17)

Cathedral Gate House, 36 Burgate, Canterbury CT1 2HA
Tel: (0227) 464381
S5 £24; D7 £44-£68; T8 £44-£68; F2 £80-£90; (prices per room); EM, PL; dogs accepted

Castle Court Guest House, 8 Castle Street, Canterbury CT1 1QF
Tel: (0227) 463441
S3 £16-£18; D5 £14-£18; T3 £14-£18; F2 £14-£18; dogs by arr.

Mrs P Banks, Hillrise, 32 Nunnery Fields, Canterbury CT1 3JT
Tel: (0227) 761758
S1 £17; T1 £33; F1 £40-£50; (prices per room); EM, PL by arr; no dogs; closed May 1994

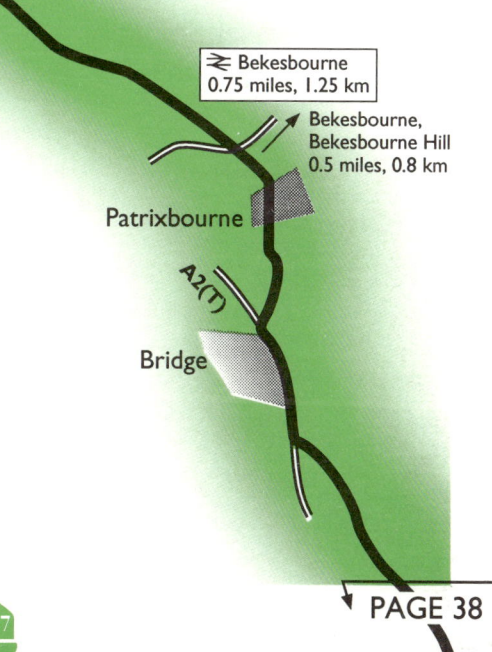

KINGSTON (TR2051)
1 mile/1.6km south
Pub: The Black Robin; PO/Gen Store; Tel; Bus Services (17, Post bus)

BARHAM (TR2050)
1 mile/1.6km south
Gen Store; PO/Gen Store; Pub: The Duke of Cumberland; Tel; Bus Services (17, Post bus)

WOMENSWOLD (TR2250)
On North Downs Way
Tel

Woodpeckers Hotel, Womenswold, Near Canterbury CT4 6HB
Tel: (0227) 831319
S3, D3, T2, F4; £25; EM, PL; flasks filled; dogs accepted

WOOLAGE VILLAGE (TR2350)
On North Downs Way
PO; Tel

WOOLAGE GREEN (TR2349)
0.5mile/0.8km south
Pub: The Two Sawyers; Tel
Mrs P Wale, Bay Tree Cottage, Woolage Green, Canterbury CT4 6SE
Tel: (0304) 830350
2 rooms; D £16 p.p.; F £50; (2 ad, 2ch); dogs by arr.

SHEPHERDSWELL (TR2648)
On North Downs Way
PO/Confectioner; Foodstore; Pubs: The Bricklayers Arms; The Bell Inn; Tel; Railway Station; Bus Services (15A, 93)

Sunshine Cottage, The Green, Mill Lane, Shepherdswell, Dover CT15 7LQ
Tel: (0304) 831359
D4 £36-£38; T2 £32-£38; F1 £36 + £10; single rate £20; EM, PL; no dogs
17th century cottage

Dover Castle

LOWER EYTHORNE (TR2849)
1 mile/1.6km north east
Pub: The White Horse
Bus Services (93, 94)

EYTHORNE (TR2849)
1 mile/1.6km north
PO/Gen Store; Fruit & Veg Shop; Pub: The Crown Inn

COLDRED (TR2747)
0.5 mile/0.8km south west
Pub: The Carpenters Arms; Tel; Bus Services (15A, 93)

WEST LANGDON (TR3247)
0.5 mile/0.8km east
Tel

GUSTON (TR3244)
0.5 mile/0.8km east
Pub: The Chance Inn; Tel; Bus Service (593)

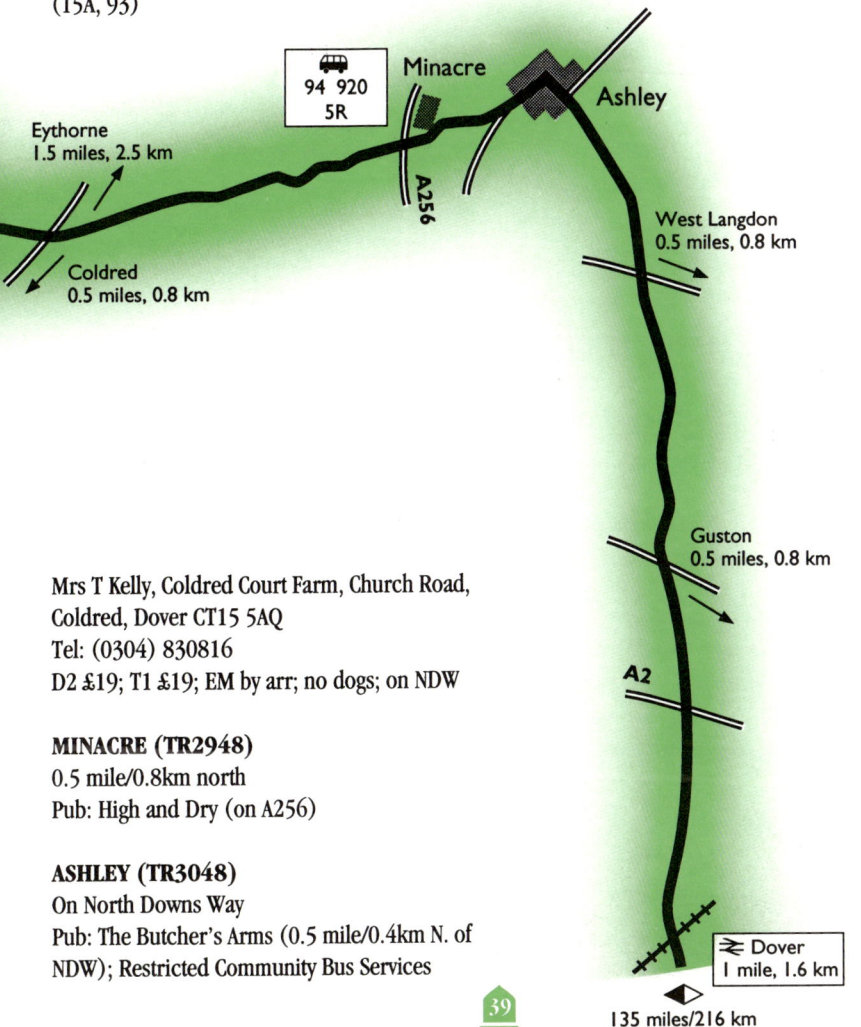

Mrs T Kelly, Coldred Court Farm, Church Road, Coldred, Dover CT15 5AQ
Tel: (0304) 830816
D2 £19; T1 £19; EM by arr; no dogs; on NDW

MINACRE (TR2948)
0.5 mile/0.8km north
Pub: High and Dry (on A256)

ASHLEY (TR3048)
On North Downs Way
Pub: The Butcher's Arms (0.5 mile/0.4km N. of NDW); Restricted Community Bus Services

ADVERTISEMENT

YHA - THE PLACE TO STAY

We offer great value, comfortable accommodation to you, your family and friends. Our facilities include tasty meals (Full breakfast £2.60, Packed Lunch £2.10 - £2.90, 3 Course Evening Meal £3.90) or self catering, drying rooms for those weather beaten days, cycle sheds, family sized rooms and much more. The Rent-a-Hostel scheme is available at Hindhead Youth Hostel during the winter months, ideal for groups wishing to take exclusive use. Joining the YHA is inexpensive and easy, find out more by contacting one of our team at the South England Regional Office, 11b York Road, Salisbury, Wiltshire SP2 7AP Tel:0722-337494 Fax:0722-414027

We regret that in the interests of safety and hygiene pets are not allowed on Youth Hostel premises.

HINDHEAD YOUTH HOSTEL
Highcoombe Bottom, Bowlhead Green, Godalming, Surrey GU7 6NS
Tel:042 860 4285

8 miles south of NDW, 16 beds, self-catering facilities only.
Under 18 £3.50 - Adult £5.30 per person, per night.
Open
April 1st - August 31st except Monday & Tuesday.
September 1st - February 28th Rent-a-Hostel

HOLMSBURY ST MARY YOUTH HOSTEL
Radnor Lane, Holmsbury St Mary, Dorking, Surrey RH5 6NW
Tel:0306-730777

2 miles south of NDW, 52 beds, full catering service & self-catering facilities available.
Under 18 £5.20 - Adult £7.75 per person, per night.
Open
February 1st - March 31st Friday & Saturday only.
April 1st - June 30th except Sunday (open Bank Holiday)

July 1st - August 31st open all time
September 1st - November 30th except Sunday & Monday
December 23rd - December 27th open for Christmas

TANNERS HATCH YOUTH HOSTEL
Polesden Lacey, Dorking, Surrey RH5 6BE
Tel:0372-452528

1 mile north of NDW, 34 beds, self-catering facilities only.
Under 18 £3.95 - Adult £5.90 per person, per night
Open
January 1st - January 4th open all time.
January 5th - February 28th except Tuesday & Wednesday
March 1st - September 30th except Tuesday
October 1st - December 20th except Tuesday & Wednesday
December 28th - January 4th '95 open for New Year

KEMSING YOUTH HOSTEL
Church Lame, Kemsing, Sevenoaks,
Kent TN15 6LU
Tel:0732-761341

½ mile south of NDW, 58 beds, full catering service & self-catering facilities available.
Under 18 £5.20 - Adult £7.75 per person, per night.
Open
February 1st - February 28th Friday & Saturday only.
March 1st - March 31st except Sunday & Monday.
April 1st - June 30th except Sunday (open Bank Holiday)
July 1st - August 31st open all time.
September 1st - October 30th except Sunday & Monday.
November 1st - December 17th Friday & Saturday only.
December 28th - January 2nd '95 open for New Year

CANTERBURY YOUTH HOSTEL
Ellerslie, 54 New Dover Road, Canterbury,
Kent CT1 3DT
Tel:0227-462911 Fax:0227-470752

72 beds, full catering service & self-catering facilities available.
Under 18 £5.80 - Adult £8.70 per person, per night.
Open
February 1st - December 30th open all time.

DOVER YOUTH HOSTEL
306 London Road, Dover, Kent CT17 0SY
Tel:0304-201314 Fax:0304-202236

134 beds, full catering service & self-catering facilities available.
Under 18 £5.80 - Adult £8.70 per person, per night.
Open
January 1st - December 31st open all time.

INDEX OF PLACES

Ashley	39	Compton	15
Barham	38	Cuxton	26
Bekesbourne	37	Detling	27
Bekesbourne Hill	37	Dorking	18
Birling	25	Dover	34
Blue Bell Hill	27	Dunley Hill Farm	17
Borough Green	24	Dunton Green	22
Botley Hill	21	East Clandon	16
Boughton Lees	31	Etchinghill	32
Box Hill	19	Eythorne	39
Boxley	27	Farnham	14
Brabourne	32	Farthing Common	32
Brasted	22	Folkestone	33
Bridge	37	Gomshall	17
Brook	31	Gravelley Hill	20
Buckland	19	Guildford	16
Burham	26	Guston	39
Canterbury	36	Halling	25
Capel-le-Ferne	34	Harrietsham	29
Caterham	20	Hastingleigh	32
Chaldon	20	Hawley's Corner	22
Charing	30	Hollingbourne	28
Chartham Hatch	36	Hucking	28
Chilham	36	Kemsing	23
Chilworth	16	Kingston	38
Chipstead	23	Knockholt	22
Coldred	39	Lenham	29

Limpsfield	20	South Hawke	20
Lower Eythorne	39	Stowting	32
Lower Kingwood	19	Sundridge	22
Lyminge	32	Tatsfield	21
Medway Towns	26	Thurnham	27
Merstham	20	Titsey	21
Minacre	39	Trottiscliffe	24
Mogador	19	Upper Halling	25
Newington	32	Vigo	24
Newlands Corner	16	West Clandon	16
Old Wives Lees	36	West Humble	18
Otford	23	West Langdon	39
Oxted	20	Westcott	18
Paddlesworth	32	Westerham	22
Pebble Coombe	19	Westwell	31
Postling	32	Whitehill	20
Puttenham	15	Womenswold	38
Reigate	19	Woolage Green	38
Reigate Hill	19	Woolage Village	38
Redhill	20	Wouldham	26
Riverhead	22	Wrotham	24
Ryarsh	25	Wye	31
The Sands	14		
Seale	14		
Shepherdswell	38		
St Catherines	15		
Shere	17		

THE COUNTRY CODE

Enjoy the countryside and respect its life and work

•

Guard against all risk of fire

•

Fasten all gates unless it stops livestock reaching their water

•

Keep your dogs under close control

•

Keep to public paths across farmland

•

Use gates and stiles to cross fences, hedges and walls

•

Leave livestock, crops and machinery alone

•

Take your litter home

•

Help to keep all water clean

•

Protect wildlife, plants and trees

•

Take special care on country roads

•

Make no unnecessary noise